K is for Kabuki

A Japan Alphabet

Written by Gloria Whelan and Jenny Nolan
Illustrated by Oki S. Han

To Maeve Hix
—Gloria

To Connor, Joe, Maeve, Keegan, Eva, and Michael
—Jenny

For Mother
—Oki

Sleeping Bear Press˙

310 North Main Street, Suite 300
Chelsea, MI 48118
www.sleepingbearpress.com

© 2009 Sleeping Bear Press is an imprint of Gale, a part of Cengage Learning.

Printed and bound in China.

First Edition

10 9 8 7 6 5 4 3 2 1

Library of Congress Cataloging-in-Publication Data on file.

Library of Congress Cataloging-in-Publication Data

Whelan, Gloria.
K is for kabuki : a Japan alphabet / written by Gloria Whelan and Jennifer
Nolan ; illustrated by Oki S. Han.
p. cm.
ISBN 978-1-58536-444-2
1. Japan—Juvenile literature. 2. English language—Alphabet—Juvenile
literature. 3. Alphabet books—Juvenile literature. I. Nolan, Jennifer. II. Han,
Oki S., ill. III. Title.
DS806.W44 2009
952—dc22
2009004807

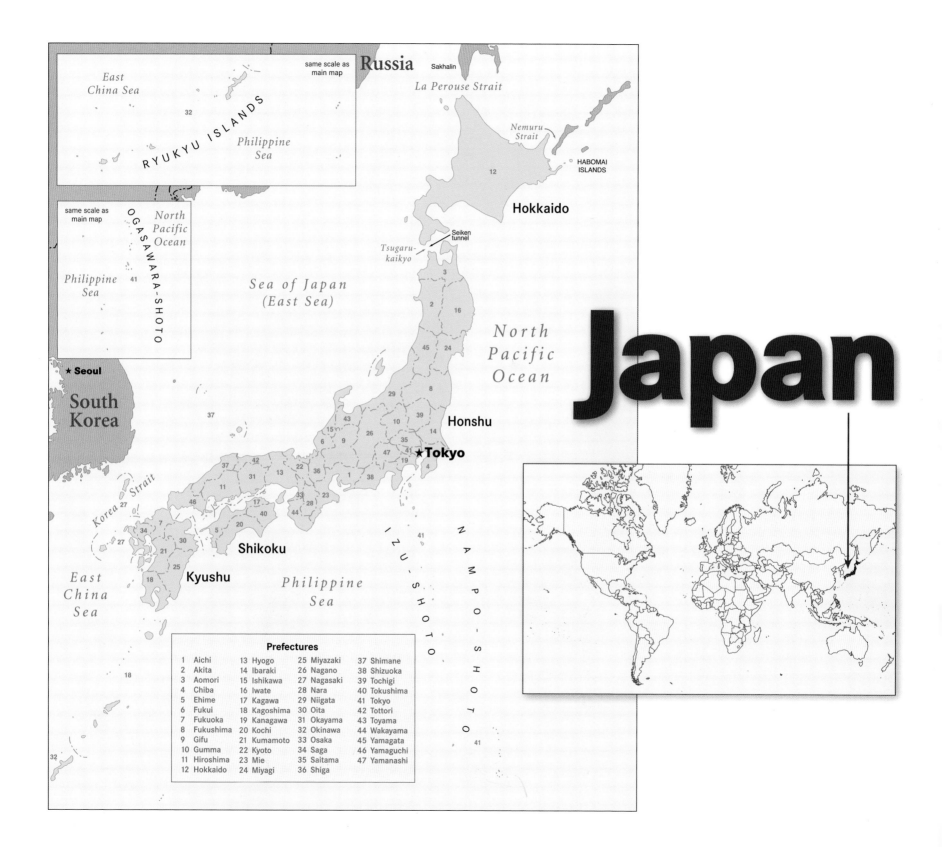

Japan

Russia

Sakhalin

La Perouse Strait

Nemuru Strait

HABOMAI ISLANDS

Hokkaido

same scale as main map

East China Sea

32

RYUKYU ISLANDS

Philippine Sea

same scale as main map

North Pacific Ocean

OGASAWARA-SHOTO

41

Philippine Sea

★ **Seoul**

South Korea

37

Sea of Japan (East Sea)

Seiken tunnel

Tsugaru-kaikyo

12

3

2

16

45

24

8

North Pacific Ocean

29

43

10

39

15

26

14

6

35

47

41

19

★ **Tokyo**

Honshu

4

42

37

31

13

22

36

1

38

11

33

23

Korea Strait

27

46

17

28

34

7

30

40

44

21

20

5

Shikoku

25

18

Kyushu

East China Sea

Philippine Sea

IZU-SHOTO

NAMPO-SHOTO

41

18

32

41

Prefectures

1 Aichi	13 Hyogo	25 Miyazaki	37 Shimane
2 Akita	14 Ibaraki	26 Nagano	38 Shizuoka
3 Aomori	15 Ishikawa	27 Nagasaki	39 Tochigi
4 Chiba	16 Iwate	28 Nara	40 Tokushima
5 Ehime	17 Kagawa	29 Niigata	41 Tokyo
6 Fukui	18 Kagoshima	30 Oita	42 Tottori
7 Fukuoka	19 Kanagawa	31 Okayama	43 Toyama
8 Fukushima	20 Kochi	32 Okinawa	44 Wakayama
9 Gifu	21 Kumamoto	33 Osaka	45 Yamagata
10 Gumma	22 Kyoto	34 Saga	46 Yamaguchi
11 Hiroshima	23 Mie	35 Saitama	47 Yamanashi
12 Hokkaido	24 Miyagi	36 Shiga	

The Akita is the national dog of Japan. The dog with erect ears and curled tail is the descendant of an ancient breed whose likeness is found carved on the early tombs of the Japanese.

In its modern form the Akita has been known since the 1700s. The dogs came from the Akita prefecture, a province on the island of Honshu. They were originally used by the aristocracy for hunting deer, bear, and wild boar. The Akita is large and dignified, and males can weigh over 100 pounds.

It is said that the dogs were so gentle and loyal that they were used as babysitters for children. The Akita was even trusted to guard the emperor and his family.

The first Akita was brought to the United States by Helen Keller, an American woman who became famous as a young girl for overcoming blindness with the help of a wonderful teacher. Keller was visiting Japan in 1937 and told her hosts how much she liked the dogs. The Japanese respected Helen Keller's triumph over her blindness and she was given an Akita named Kamikaze-go. Sadly, before he was a year old he died, but his brother Kenzan-go was sent to replace him, and lived happily in Connecticut with Keller for many years.

A is for Akita

With curly tail and gentle ways
Akita won the emperor's praise.
An ancient dog, tried and true,
from the isle of far Honshu.

Hachiko is the most famous Akita. There is a life-sized bronze statue of him at the Shibuya Station in Tokyo. Hachiko's master was an agriculture professor at the University of Tokyo. His name was Ueno Hidesamuroh. Hachiko would see the professor off in the morning from his front door and then go to the Shibuya train station each evening to meet Ueno Hidesamuroh when he came home from work. The professor died in 1925, but Hachiko, for the rest of his life, continued to return to the train station every day to wait for his master. This story of devotion is often told to Japanese children as an example of family loyalty.

Bb

B is for Bullet Train

The train passes the rabbit and deer;
the train passes the falcon and crow.
Riders from Mutsu to Mito
praise Shima the engineer.

Japan is very crowded, and cars are not practical for travel so the Japanese decided to make their train system quick and easy.

In 1964 the Japanese opened the bullet train line, the world's first high-speed train. The fastest trains in the world, they have gone up to 277 miles per hour. In Japanese, the train is called *Shinkansen*.

Shima Hideo was the engineer who designed the bullet train. The construction of the *Shinkansen* system required the building of 3,000 bridges and 67 tunnels. It cost so much money, Shima Hideo lost his job! However, Hideo, who lived to be 96, was later honored throughout Japan for his achievement.

More than six billion passengers have ridden on the *Shinkansen*! No one has ever died from a train crash or derailment, even during earthquakes or bad storms. The trains cross the whole country, from the north all the way down to Tokyo.

The longest trains are a quarter-mile long, but when they pull into the station, they always end up exactly at the right place. The average bullet train arrival time is within six seconds of its schedule.

Forests cover two-thirds of Japan, but the most famous tree in Japan is the cherry tree (called *sakura*). In the spring the Japanese Meteorological Agency announces the *Sakura Zensen*, Cherry Blossom Front, predicting the date of the first bloom of the trees.

There are parties and picnics to celebrate. A flower viewing party is called a *Hanami*. There are guides on how to view the blossoms!

Even the fierce *samurai* warriors felt a bond with the cherry blossoms because the blossoms symbolize a graceful death. The fallen blossoms are said to be like fallen warriors who die bravely in battle. The blossoms are a reminder that life is fleeting and so should be lived beautifully.

In 1912 the Japanese people gave 3,000 cherry trees to the United States to cement the friendship between our two countries. The trees were planted around the Tidal Basin in Washington, D.C. Cherry blossom time in the capital brings visitors from all over the country. During World War II, many of Japan's cherry trees were destroyed, so in 1952 the United States gave to Japan a gift of cherry trees, descendants of the same trees Japan had sent to us.

C is for Cherry Blossom

The cherry blossom trembles in the breeze,
it lasts but one short day,
a lesson for the Japanese
that even beauty fades away.

Japanese theater has ancient roots. It is meant to be seen, rather than read, so its meaning comes from the movement of the actors on the stage. *No* or *Noh* drama originated in the fourteenth century. *Noh* means skill or accomplishment. A man named Kan'ami took lessons in early music called *sarugaku* (which means monkey music!). He wrote plays incorporating the music into a stylized drama whose actors wore masks.

Noh actors are traditionally male, even those who play women's roles. Their masks and costumes tell the story of the characters. There are just two actors. The actors chant, or sing in a monotone. The plays are short, but take a long time to perform because the actors move very slowly.

There is a chorus on the side of the stage, and musicians in the background who play traditional instruments. A *Noh* actor starts training at a very young age, sometimes younger than five years old!

Kyogen is another form of drama. *Kyogen* means "mad words." *Kyogen* are often performed between *Noh* plays to make the audience laugh.

D is for Drama

The Noh actor plays hide and seek
behind a mask that covers his face.
He chants or sings but never speaks
as he moves with leisurely grace.

In the sixteenth and seventeenth centuries another form of drama, called *Kabuki*, became popular. *Kabuki* was started by a woman, Okuni, who danced to make money for the Izumo shrine where her father worked. Women were the initial actors in *Kabuki* drama, but eventually the men took over.

Kabuki is colorful and full of spectacle. There are trap doors where actors disappear, and sometimes the stage revolves. Actors wear elaborate makeup and the costumes can weigh as much as fifty pounds!

Bunraku is a theater with puppets. The plays are accompanied by a traditional musical instrument called a *shamisen*, with three strings like a banjo. A chanter sits next to the puppets and recites the speaking parts.

The puppeteer, called an *omozukai*, is visible to the audience. He trains for ten years as an apprentice to a master puppeteer. The puppets are two to four feet tall and are controlled by a handle that comes down from the neck of the puppet.

Ee

Japan's government is a constitutional monarchy. It is run by a Parliament called the Diet. It consists of the House of Councilors and the House of Representatives. Both houses are elected by the people. The Diet then elects the Prime Minister.

Japan also has an emperor who holds the title of Head of the Country, even though he doesn't have any say in what the government does. The constitution calls him "the symbol of the state and the unity of the people." The emperor lives in the Imperial Palace in Tokyo. The palace is surrounded by a moat and beautiful gardens.

The first modern emperor was Meiji who ruled from 1867 to 1912. Before Meiji, the *shogun*, who were like feudal lords, controlled the emperor but Meiji took the power away from the *shogun* and wrote a constitution.

The current emperor's name is Akihito, and he became emperor when his father, Hirohito, died in 1989. Akihito is an expert on the taxonomy of gobioid fishes and has published over two dozen papers on the subject. Akihito married Michiko, who was not a princess, but a commoner—the first commoner to marry a Japanese emperor.

E is for Emperor

In his garden where he goes for a stroll
the beauty of the flowers stirs the emperor's soul.
He gazes into the water of the moat,
a fish swims by and he makes a note.

F f

F is for Fujisan

People and cars and noise all about me,
I'm a little boat tossed in an angry sea.
Clouds part with the sun to show me Mt. Fuji,
peace comes like a gift and makes me carefree.

San is the Japanese word for "mountain" and Mount Fuji is the highest and most famous mountain in Japan. Shaped like a perfect cone and mantled with snow, Mt. Fuji's grandeur has inspired many writers and artists.

Over 80% of the countryside of Japan is mountainous or hilly and not habitable. That is why the cities have so many people. Mt. Fuji is about 60 miles west of Tokyo and can be seen on a clear day. Its nearness to the city makes the mountain more appreciated because its beauty and majesty are such a contrast to the busy city.

The Japanese revere nature, and Mt. Fuji is regarded as a sacred object. The Japanese people have a folk tradition centered around the mountains called *sangaku shinko* which means spiritual beliefs connected to sacred mountains.

Climbing Fujisan is regarded by some as a religious experience. The official climbing season is summer when the mountain is mostly free of snow and mountain huts are open. Climbers can pay to reserve a bed. Many climbers try to time their climb to see the sun rise from the summit of the mountain.

Tokyo was formerly a fishing village called Edo set amidst an estuary formed by three rivers. By 1600 the *shogun* at that time had made Edo his center of power. In 1869 when Emperor Meiji took back power, he renamed the city *Tokyo* which means "Eastern Capital."

Of Japan's 47 prefectures (provinces), Tokyo is the most populated. Home of the government and the emperor, it serves as Japan's capital. There are approximately eight million people in Tokyo proper and thirty-five million people in the metropolitan area.

Tokyo is famous for its shopping areas. One called Akihabara has thousands of stores that sell computers, televisions, cell phones, cameras, and everything electronic.

Tsukiji is the largest fish market in the world, selling 2,000 tons of fish each day.

Tokyo's most famous shopping area is called the Ginza. Under the *shogun* a government mint was built there to make silver coins. The Japanese word "Ginza" comes from the meaning of *gin-* silver and *za-*guild. After a large fire in 1872, Ginza was rebuilt by European architects as a part of Emperor Meiji's effort to modernize Japan. Ginza has large department stores as well as small exclusive shops and galleries. It also has many nightclubs and restaurants.

Gg

G is for Ginza

What shall we buy, a shark or a cod,
a painting or shoes or a fishing rod,
a camera, a cell phone, a stylish dress,
a diamond, a chair, or a set of chess?

池や蛙飛びこむ水の音

H is for Haiku

The careless frog jumps
in the pond without looking
the heron's cruel beak.

Poetry is important in Japanese culture. Even the fierce *samurai* warriors wrote poetry. Emperors and the nobility wrote poetry all the time. Emperor Meiji is said to have written 100,000 poems!

The most popular forms of traditional poetry are *waka* and *haiku*. *Waka* has five lines and *haiku*, three. The *haiku* must have seventeen syllables, five in the first line, seven in the second, and five in the last. A *haiku* captures a moment in time, often using an image from nature to explain something about life. There is usually a pause in the poem that lets the reader think about what might follow. *Haiku*, like other Japanese poetry, do not rhyme. *Haiku* is used as both the singular and plural form.

Matsuo Bashō (1644 -1694) is a famous writer of *haiku*. Bashō wrote a *haiku* about a frog (the Japanese version has the correct number of syllables):

An ancient pond
A frog jumps in
A splash of water.

This frog *haiku* became so popular that other poets started a *renga*, a game or competition where one poet starts a poem and another finishes it. All the poems in the *renga* were about frogs!

I is for Island

The islands have the deer and the fox,
the otter, the mink, and the ox,
the walrus, the wolf, and the hare
and the overly curious bear.

Hokkaido

Honshu

Kyushu *Shikoku*

Japan is a series of islands: four large ones (Hokkaido, Honshu, Shikoku, and Kyushu) and over three thousand small ones. Wherever you live in Japan you are never farther than 90 miles from the sea.

Because it is so close to the sea, Japan's climate is mild. Spring and autumn are sunny and clear. Summers are humid and hot. Only the northern and western parts of Japan and the higher elevations see much snow.

Forests cover two-thirds of Japan. There are fir trees as well as birch, oak, and maple, and in the warmer sections of the country acres and acres of bamboo. Wolves and raccoons live in the forests; mink, seals, and walrus along the rivers and the sea. There are both black bears and brown bears in Japan. The bears are not at all shy and sometimes lumber into the outskirts of Tokyo.

With its population of over 127 million, Japan has the world's tenth largest population, but as a highly industrialized country it is the second largest consumer of energy in the world, right after the United States. This is a problem for Japan because it has no oil reserves and must rely on other countries to supply its needs.

I i

During the period of the *shogun* and the *samurai* in Japan, martial arts were practiced by all of the *samurai*. In addition to horsemanship and skill with swords and other weapons, the *samurai* learned an ancient art of hand-to-hand combat called *jujitsu*. *Jujitsu* is weaponless fighting. Practitioners use holds and throws to disable their opponent. The literal definition of *jujitsu* is the art of "softness."

When Japan became unified in the 1600s, fighting with weapons became rarer, and the art of *jujitsu* was perfected. The schools that taught it began to allow merchants and other people who were not *samurai* to learn this hand-to-hand combat.

By the late 1880s *judo* had become hugely popular. *Judo* means "gentle way" and is practiced now all over the world. The words "gentle" and "softness" do not mean that *judo* or *jujitsu* combatants are soft or gentle! They refer to the fact that an expert in one of these arts does not attack, but uses the force and energy of his attacker against him.

Judo became an Olympic sport in 1964, when Japan hosted the Olympics. The host country of the Olympics was allowed to add one sport, and Japan chose *judo*.

J is for Jujitsu and Judo

The samurai stretches out his hand;
the enemy doesn't understand.
We're not talking friendship here
but something rather more severe.

K k

Most Japanese people wear western-style clothes for everyday. Kids wear jeans and usually a uniform at school. Men wear business suits to work, and women like designer clothes. But on ceremonial days, and for formal occasions, *kimono* are traditional in Japan for both men and women. The word *kimono* means "something to wear." (*Kimono* is used as both the singular and plural form.)

Kimono have been worn since the late sixth century. Elaborate wedding *kimono* are sometimes handed down through the family. They are white for the wedding ceremony and a patterned silk brocade *kimono* is worn over the white one for the reception.

Both women and men tie an *obi* (sash) around their *kimono*. The men's *obi* is narrow. The women's *obi*—actually three different belts on top of each other—is wider and very elaborate. Sometimes, particularly for a wedding, a professional *kimono* arranger will tie the *obi*. The bow is worn in the back and there are many different ways to tie it. One is called *cho-cho*, the word for butterfly, because the bow resembles butterfly wings. *Kimono* are worn with split-toe socks called *tabi* and sandals called *gela* or *zori*.

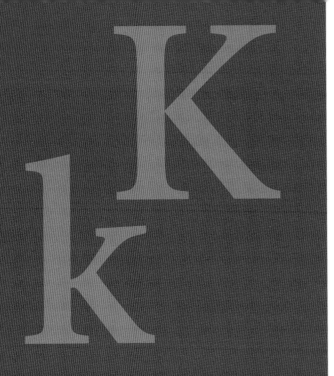

K is for Kimono

The kimono of the bride
is the family's pride,
the white silk gown
tradition handed down.

Wherever you look in Japan you will find lanterns. There are stone and iron lanterns in gardens and temples. There are paper lanterns everywhere. There is a festival in Japan called *Obon* (or *Bon* for short) that involves lanterns. *Obon* is held in summer and is the Buddhist celebration of ancestors. All over Japan, people return to their home-towns. Buddhist families decorate their altars with paper lanterns called *chouchin*. The families light the lanterns in their houses and then go to the graves of their ancestors to invite their spirits to return back home with them. On the last night of *Obon*, people set lighted paper lanterns afloat in rivers to guide back their ancestors' spirits.

There are many more festivals in Japan. New Year's Day (*Shogatsu*) is a big holiday. Offices are closed. Each new year in Japan is seen as a fresh start, so that in December people hurry to finish any outstanding tasks. New Year parties, *bonenkai*, are held to celebrate finishing up the previous year's duties and forgetting any unpleasantness or troubles from the previous year. Buddhist temples toll their bells 108 times, symbol-izing the driving out of the 108 mortal desires that torment humans.

L
1

L is for Lantern

Lanterns in the treetops high,
lanterns glowing like a firefly.
For the ancestors who roam,
lanterns show the long way home.

Coming of Age Day follows New Year's and is celebrated on the second Monday of January. On this day twenty-year-olds become adults and can vote or marry without parental permission.

In February, when everyone is looking forward to spring, there is a festival called *Setsubun*. It is a celebration of the division between winter and spring. On this festival day, the doors and windows are opened and the male head of the household throws roasted soybeans out the door. This is meant to drive away the evil spirits so that good luck can enter. At the temples, the priests do the same thing.

In March, there is the Doll's Festival or *Hina Matsuri*, also known as Girl's Day. Girls display their Hina dolls made especially for Doll's Festival. Hina dolls have porcelain faces and cloth bodies dressed in beautiful costumes. Some families have dolls that are very old and have been handed down through generations. Girls wear their best *kimono* and invite friends and family over to view their dolls and have tea and cakes.

Hundreds of years ago, Japanese artists created scrolls that told a story with pictures and some text to explain the action. Today, *manga*, the Japanese word for comics, are read by everyone from businessmen on their way to work to young girls after school. The city of Hiroshima has a public library dedicated exclusively to *manga*!

Manga are so popular in Japan that they make up approximately 22% of all printed material. The comics are mostly in black and white and are serialized, printed in huge, thick magazines and collected into books. The serials go on for months, sometimes for years. There are *manga* for boys (*shonen*) and for girls (*shojo*). Both men and women create the *manga*. There is a similarity of style that runs throughout much of the *manga*: characters have large eyes and big or wild hair.

Manga can be informational, explaining science or a governmental regulation. They can be historical and many of the *manga* describe the exploits of the *samurai*. They can be about sports, some even tell the story of a play by Shakespeare. The Japanese *manga* stories are not always about super-heroes like American comics are. They are often about ordinary people who get caught up in an adventure.

M is for Manga

Brave Romeo, and his big hair,
with Juliet makes a handsome pair.
When poor Romeo sadly dies,
tears fall from Juliet's big eyes.

Very popular *manga* are often made into an animated film (*anime*). One popular *anime* is "Sailor Moon," about teenage girls who battle evil. The sailor part of their names comes from girls' school uniforms (common in Japan) that look like sailor shirts. The girls are named after the moon and planets. The series started out as *manga*, and was made into *anime* and video games. Another popular series from Japan and famous in America as well, is the Pokemon series which started as a Game Boy, then was made into *manga* and *anime*. Countries all over the world are adopting the *manga* style and *manga* comics.

The Japanese put the family name (last name) first, followed by the personal name (first name). Instead of Sally Smith, it would be Smith Sally.

Instead of Mr. or Mrs. at the beginning of the last name, the Japanese use -san as a designation of respect. When you are introduced to a man, you would call him Masuda-san, which would mean Mr. Masuda.

In ancient times, only the nobility or military families had last names. Common people had only first names, often taken from what the person did for a living, or where they came from.

When a child is born, much thought is given to his or her first name. Parents look for favorable meanings. The character that makes up the first name is often the name of a flower or a positive trait like sincerity (*Makoto*) or truth (*Tadashi*). Names are usually formed by combining two characters. The characters for beauty and summer would be put together to make the name, Beautiful Summer.

Seimei Handan is a system of traditional fortune-telling which some parents consult before naming their children. It uses the number of brush strokes in the name's written Japanese characters to decide if it is a name that foretells a good future for the child.

N is for Names

She is born as summer ends
with a nature that portends
a peaceful child, so we'll proclaim
Gentle Autumn is her name.

O o

O is for Origami

A paper frog, a paper tree,
a paper sunflower just for me,
a paper fox, a paper shrew,
a paper tiger just for you.

Japanese people have made paper for over a thousand years. They use it for beautiful art and also in their homes. Walls and screens are made out of paper. The Japanese make huge paper kites to fly. On a smaller scale there is *origami*.

Origami is the art of paper folding. Children learn it in school. Square pieces of paper are folded into shapes that resemble birds, butterflies, animals, or flowers. The paper isn't cut or pasted or taped, just cleverly folded to make the desired shape.

Special paper is sold just for *origami*. It is crisp and holds the sharp folds. The paper comes in many different colors. Accomplished *origami* artists can make their folded creatures with moving parts, so that a bird's wings flap when its tail is pulled or a frog hops, when a special spot is pressed.

If you would like to learn *origami*, there is a Web site (paperfolding.com) that will show you how. The Web site has pictures of cranes that flap their wings, dinosaurs, a frog on a lily pad, and a clock that ticks.

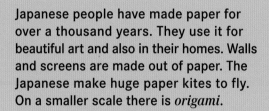

The earliest pottery in Japan, as well as elsewhere in the known world, was decorated by pressing ropes into the clay, or coiling the clay to look like roping. The pots were made for cooking as well as the storage of seeds and grain. The women who made the pots wanted them to be beautiful as well as useful.

After the introduction of the tea ceremony into Japan, a new kind of pottery was created. It was called *raku* pottery. The clay used was found near the old imperial city of Kyoto. Legend says that the emperor bestowed a seal upon the son of the first *raku* maker, Tanaka Chōjirō. The seal used the word *raku*, which translates as "pleasure."

Raku tea bowls are very plain. The bowls are fired at a low temperature and taken out of the kiln while still hot. Sometimes the bowls are put into water to cool them. When the bowls cool rapidly, it creates a special color and texture. Because the tea bowls are handmade and each one is different, the potters often gave their creations names. Today *raku* pottery is made all over the world using a method invented 500 years ago in Japan.

P is for Pottery

On an ordinary day
as a woman molds the clay,
inspiration moves her hand,
bringing beauty to the land.

Fabrics and textiles have always been an important part of Japanese culture. Gorgeous floral silks and brocades are made into elegant *kimono*. But Japanese homes are much simpler in their decorating style than American or European homes. Quilts made by Japanese women for their home tend to be simpler than American quilts.

In Japan the emphasis is on the elegance of the stitching. The stitching of quilts is called *sashiko*. *Sashiko* originated many hundreds of years ago as a way to make clothing warmer and sturdier.

European knights in the Middle Ages who traveled to the East picked up the Asian idea of quilted clothing to wear under their armor for protection and warmth. They brought the art of quilting back to Europe and eventually it traveled to America.

The usual background for *sashiko* quilting is an indigo-colored fabric. Indigo is a blue color, and can range from light to very dark. The threads in *sashiko* are white, and the distinctive look of the white stitching on the blue fabric is what makes classic *sashiko*. Many designs for *sashiko* are taken from nature—animals, clouds, and bamboo. These designs can have colorful names like "Rising Steam" or "Seven Treasures of Buddha."

Q is for Quilting

She hears the cold winds blow,
she sees the falling snow.
There's no need for alarm,
her quilt will keep her warm.

Rr

R is for Religion

I'll be a kami that swims in the sea
or I'll glow in the moon from afar.
I'll be a kami perched high in a tree
or a kami that shines in a star.

Japan's two major religions are Buddhism and Shinto. Shinto, which means "Way of the Gods," is native to Japan. *Kami* are spirits that live in nature and in Shinto shrines. *Kami* can be in the moon, the stars, mountains and rivers, waterfalls and winds, seas and rocks.

One of the most important *kami* is Amaterasu, the Sun Goddess. A legend tells that Amaterasu was appointed to rule over the heavens and her brother, Susanoo, was to rule over the sea. Susanoo was very mischievous and played tricks on his sister. The Sun Goddess became so angry with her brother she withdrew into a cave and the whole world became dark. The other deities in the heavens tried to lure her out with a celebration. They placed a rooster on a *torii* (a bird perch) to crow as a signal the celebration was going to begin. When Amaterasu peeked out to see what was going on, the *kami* pulled her all the way out of the cave and once again there was light. Now every Shinto shrine has at least one *torii* as a gateway to the shrine. It is composed of two leaning, upright supports, with two bars across the top.

Visitors to the Shinto shrines leave *omikuji*, little slips of paper. Tying the *omikuji* to a tree is a way of asking for good fortune to come or for bad fortune not to happen.

Buddhism is the religion practiced by most Japanese. Gautama Siddhārtha was a prince born in the sixth century in India. He did not understand why there was so much suffering in the world. To find the answer he gave up his riches and his comfortable life to live in poverty and simplicity and to meditate. He discovered all suffering is caused by desire, hatred, and ignorance. When he understood this, he became known as Buddha, the Enlightened One.

There are many temples in Japan dedicated to Buddha. The largest wooden building in the world is a temple to Buddha in the city of Nara. Inside the temple is a statue of Buddha 53 feet tall, made of bronze and 290 pounds of gold.

In the twelfth century the emperor called in his warriors to put down a series of uprisings. The chief of the warriors was Minamoto Yoritomo. Yoritomo, known as the *shogun*, became so powerful that he took over the government from the emperor. The *shogun* ruled Japan for hundreds of years. Although he had no power under the *shogun*, the emperor was allowed to remain on his throne.

The *shogun* had lords, known as *daimyo*, who were loyal to him. The *daimyo*, in turn, had warriors in their employ called *samurai*. The *samurai* were not like regular soldiers, but more like European medieval knights, ready to give up their lives for their lords.

Like feudal knights, the *samurai* were well educated and wrote poetry. They lived by a code of honor called *Bushidō* (the way of the warrior). They honored virtue and duty.

In 1867 the *samurai* rose up against the *shogun* and restored Emperor Meiji to power. It was the beginning of the end for the *samurai's* power. Meiji began to open Japan to the West, adopting the western style of industrialization. As Japan became more modern, the *samurai*, who began as a protective force for their lords, were no longer needed to keep peace.

S is for Samurai

Feeling a little bored
the samurai puts down his sword,
picks up a pen to record
his bravery for his lord.

Japan began using tea around the eighth century. It came from China, and at first was for medicinal purposes. In the six-teenth century, a man named Sen no Rikyu changed the Japanese way of thinking about tea ceremonies. Sen no Rikyu believed that each meeting between people was unique and could never occur again in exactly the same way. Therefore, it should be treasured. His four principles were: harmony, respect, purity, and tranquility.

Rikyu simplified everything. Though the utensils of the tea ceremony are simple, the practice of the ceremony is a very complex art form. Tea masters study for years to perfect their technique. They must know about *kimono* and flowers and different kinds of tea and ceramics.

The tea ceremony (known as *chado*) begins with guests washing their hands and rinsing their mouths from a basin in the garden, then walking up a *roji* (dewy path), entering the tea house through a low doorway. They remove their shoes before entering.

T is for Tea Ceremony

Noon sun shines brightly.
The tea ceremony ends
when the moon rises.

The tea house is rustic in style to evoke nature. The ceremony is meant to be an escape from busy everyday life to a place of beauty and serenity. The guests are quiet when inside the tea room, admiring the decorations which may be one vase of flowers, or a scroll on the wall. They enjoy the sound of the water and the fire, and the smells of the incense and tea.

The host makes the tea very formally using a special scoop and whisk. A meal may be served, or just sweets, and then the tea itself is served. There are very exact rules that must be followed: how the cups can be held, or the way the tea is stirred. The host offers the first bowl of tea to the most important guest, and they bow to each other. That guest then bows to the guest who is second in importance, and so on. After the guests have finished their tea, the host washes the utensils and offers them to the guests who admire them and return them to the host. As the guests leave, the host bows to them from the door, and the ceremony is over. Tea ceremonies can take up to four or five hours, a true escape from the busy outside world.

U is for Ukiyo-e

A leaf tumbles from a tree,
a fish jumps in the sea,
gone in a moment's rush,
caught by the artist's brush.

Early Japanese art reflected Buddhist themes and was displayed in temples. Later, secular subjects, mostly of nature, were painted on scrolls. The scrolls were unrolled and appreciated a little at a time.

At the same time a style of Japanese painting, *Ukiyo-e*, was developing. *Ukiyo-e* means "pictures of the floating world." Although many of the paintings depicted water, the art expressed the thought that life is fleeting, that it can pass us by like something that floats by on a river.

Japan's best known art is its woodblock prints. Artists carve blocks of wood and put ink on them, pressing them onto sheets of paper to make beautiful pictures. At first only one block and one color was used, requiring the artist to paint the other colors on each print. Then it was discovered that by using several blocks, many inexpensive prints could be made.

Ando Hiroshige, who lived from 1797 to 1858, is considered to be a master of the woodblock print. Hiroshige did a series of prints called, "Fifty-three Stations on the Tokaido Road." The Tokaido was a road between Edo and Kyoto. People used his prints like postcards for souvenirs of their trip.

Uu

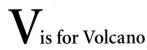

V is for Volcano

The sea's smooth surface hides
the plate's rude shifts and slides
and in this deadly hour
    displays the earth's cruel power.

Japan is a mountainous country, and many of those mountains are volcanoes. A volcano is caused by an opening in the earth allowing lava (hot molten rock) and ash to rise from below the earth's crust. Over the ages the lava and ash cool and harden to create a mountain. Millions of years ago, Japan itself rose from the sea as underground plates shifted, causing the earth's crust to rise above the ocean. These plates are still moving and knocking together.

Japan has more than 250 volcanoes. Approximately 108 of the volcanoes are active volcanoes, which mean they may erupt, and many do, sometimes spewing ash or mud or lava. Although it has not erupted since 1706, Mt. Fuji is still categorized as an active volcano.

Japan has around 1,500 earthquakes a year, but many of them are small. The worst earthquake in recent memory was the Great Kanto earthquake of 1923. It destroyed the cities of Tokyo and Yokohama. Almost 150,000 people died in that tragedy.

Present-day Japan works very hard to predict its earthquakes and to make sure that buildings and trains are safe from the quakes.

W is for Wasabi

The sushi chef proudly presents the plate
of halibut, tuna, salmon, and skate.
Each morsel a triumph of beauty and skill
and the fish very fresh so it doesn't kill.

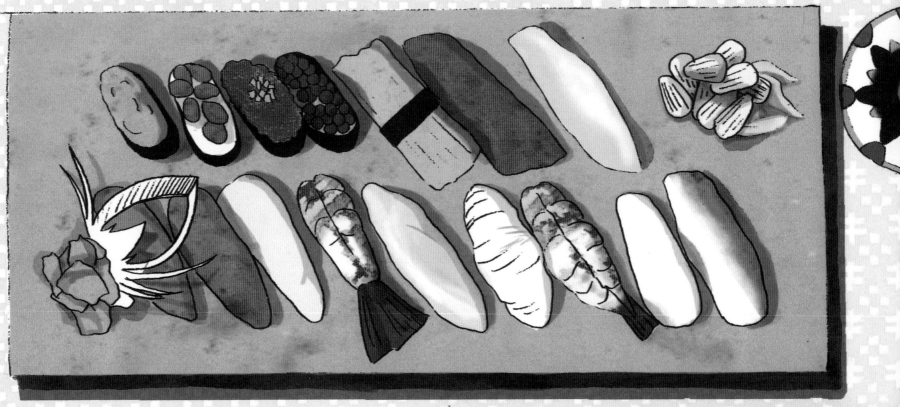

Japanese wasabi is a hot, spicy, green paste, similar to horseradish. It is made from the wasabi plant which is a root vegetable. Japanese people eat wasabi with *sushi* and *sashimi*, raw fish eaten in restaurants and *sushi* bars.

Sushi is everywhere in Japan. It consists of raw fish wrapped in rice, dipped in soy sauce, and garnished with wasabi. *Sashimi* is raw fish, but without the rice. Because Japan is surrounded by ocean and fishing is an important industry, the fish is so fresh that it is safe to eat it raw.

Sushi chefs have a long training period. They have to learn to recognize the different kinds of fish and know if the fish is fresh. They have to be able to cut the fish artistically and create delicate rolls of rice and fish.

Traditional Japanese homes and restaurants have low tables. Diners sit on a mat or cushions on the floor. Men sit cross-legged, women have their legs to the side. Japanese do not wear their shoes in the house; they are taken off just inside the front door of the house, and in a traditional restaurant they take off their shoes before they are seated in the dining area.

W
W

Xx

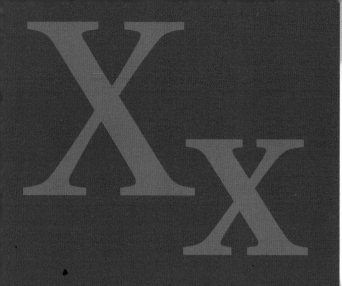

There is no **X** in the Japanese alphabet, even when they use Roman letters as we do. There are three alphabets for the Japanese language: *Kanji* (which are Chinese characters); *Kana*; and *Romaji* (which are letters like ours used for international business and tourism).

Grammar is simple in Japanese. There is no difference between plural and singular or masculine and feminine. A sentence usually begins with the topic or object instead of a pronoun: "he likes the book" would be "the book—he likes it."

Japanese is written in columns that read from top to bottom and right- to left-hand order. Books in Japan open from the left side, and you start reading them from what to us would be the back!

Many words in the Japanese language convey respect and the Japanese are very courteous in addressing one another.

Here are some Japanese words:

Please: *douzo*
Thank you: *arigato*
Hello: *kon-nichiwa*
How are you?: *o-genki desu ka*
What is your name?: *anata no namae wa nan to iimasu ka?*
Nice to meet you: *o-ai dekite ureshii desu*
Goodbye: *sayounara*

X is for the Letter That Isn't

The Japanese wish to please,
in all they say they find a way
to show they know
polite is right.

Yen is the name of Japan's currency. The smallest bill is a one-thousand yen note. There are coins as small as one yen. The pictures on the yen notes honor cultural heroes, like Higuchi Ichiyo, a woman novelist, and places of beauty like Mt. Fuji.

Japan is a great manufacturing country. They make cars and electronics like computers and cell phones and video games that sell all over the world.

Agriculture and fishing are also important industries. The Japanese grow about 40% of what they eat. The rest has to be imported because of the Japanese terrain, which is mountainous. Rice is the largest crop in Japan because it can be grown not only in fields but on terraced hillsides.

The Japanese have been fishermen for thousands of years. The Japanese eat a lot of fish, which is one of the reasons they are such a healthy country. They also export fish to other countries.

After the dollar and the euro, the yen is the most traded currency in the world.

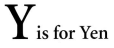

Y is for Yen

On the roads of Japan see the trendy Toyota,
the Nissan and Mazda and the hybrid Volta.
You'll find Acura and Honda and Subaru;
Mitsubishi and Lexus and here comes Isuzu.

In Japan, landscape, gardens, and architecture are all interrelated and show the love of the Japanese people for their country and nature. One of the Japanese words for garden, *niwa*, means "a place of purification for the spirits." Japanese gardens are often composed of rocks, pebbles, and sand. They are referred to as "Zen Gardens" because the Zen sect of Buddhism perfected this art. The garden at the Zen temple of Ryoan-ji, meaning "Temple of the Peaceful Dragon," is more than 500 years old.

Zen emphasizes nature, simplicity, and meditation. The rock gardens are meant to be used as an aid to contemplation: there are no bright colors, no distracting bushes and hedges, just the simplicity of the stones. In the rock gardens, pebbles, or sometimes sand, represent the sea or a river, and the larger rocks represent the islands or mountains that rise out of the sea, like the mountains and islands of Japan itself.

People do not walk through rock gardens; the gardens are meant to be looked at from a viewing area or a building. Japanese houses have large walls of windows. There are screens and shutters that are used to show different views of the gardens at different times of the day.

Z is for Zen Gardens

Looking out the window
you see the river flow,
sand that doesn't blow
pebbles in a row.

Glossary

Pronunciation tips:
- Syllables are *not* accented in the Japanese language, all get equal emphasis.
- Kyo is pronounced as one syllable, like the **cu** of *cure*, but with the 'o' sound instead of u.
- G is always the hard 'g' as in *good*.
- TS is pronounced together like the **ts** in *hot soup*.

anime (ah-nee-may): manga made into an animated film (Please see letter M)

bonenkai (boh-nen-kye): New Year parties (Please see letter L)

Buddhism (boo-diz-im): one of Japan's two major religions (Please see letter R)

Bunraku (bun-rah-koo): a theatrical production using puppets (Please see letter D)

Bushidō (boo-shee-doh): the samurai code of honor (Please see letter S)

chado (chah-doh): the study of the traditional ceremonial way to serve tea (Please see letter T)

cho-cho (choh-choh): a type of bow tied with the obi sash, *cho-cho* is Japanese for butterfly (Please see letter K)

chouchin (chow-chin): paper lanterns used by Buddhist families to decorate their altars (Please see letter L)

daimyo (dye-meoh): lords who were loyal to the shogun (Please see letter S)

gela (geh-lah): traditional sandals, also called *zori* (Please see letter K)

Ginza (gin-zah): the Japanese word for silver mint (Please see letter G)

haiku (hye-koo): a form of poetry utilizing three lines and seventeen syllables (Please see letter H)

Hanami (hah-nah-mee): a party or gathering to view the cherry blossoms (Please see letter C)

Hina Matsuri (hee-na mah-tsu-ree): a festival held in March, called the Doll's Festival or Girl's Day (Please see letter L)

jujitsu (joo-jit-soo): weaponless, hand-to-hand way of fighting (Please see letter J)

Kabuki (kah-boo-kee): a form of drama from the sixteenth and seventeenth centuries (Please see letter D)

kami (kah-mee): spirits that live in nature and in Shinto shrines (Please see letter R)

Kana (kah-nah): phonetic characters in the Japanese written language (Please see letter X)

Kanji (kan-jee): Chinese characters used in the Japanese writing system (Please see letter X)

kimono (kee-moh-noh): a traditional garment worn for ceremonies and formal occasions (Please see letter K)

Kyogen (kyoh-gehn): a form of humorous drama (Please see letter D)

manga (mahn-gah): the Japanese word for comics (Please see letter M)

niwa (nee-wah): a Japanese word for garden (Please see letter Z)

No or **Noh** (noh): a form of drama that originated in the fourteenth century (Please see letter D)

obi (oh-bee): the sash tied around the waist of a kimono (Please see letter K)

Obon (oh-bahn): a Buddhist festival held in summer that celebrates ancestors (Please see letter L)

omikuji (oh-mee-koo-jee): little slips of paper left at Shinto shrines asking for good fortune (Please see letter R)

omozukai (oh-moh-zoo-kye): the puppeteer in Bunraku theater (Please see letter D)

origami (oh-ree-gah-mee): the art of paper folding (Please see letter O)

raku (rah-koo): a type of simple clay pottery often used in tea ceremonies (Please see letter P)

renga (ren-gah): a game or competition where one poet starts a poem and another finishes it (Please see letter H)

roji (roh-jee): a garden path leading to a tea house (Please see letter T)

Romaji (roh-mah-jee): the Japanese alphabet with Roman letters (Please see letter X)

samurai (sah-moo-rye): warriors who were employed by the daimyo (Please see letter S)

Sakura Zensen (sah-koo-rah zen-sen): the name for the Cherry Blossom Front (Please see letter C)

sarugaku (sah-roo-gah-koo): a form of early Japanese music (Please see letter D)

san (sahn): the Japanese word for mountain (Please see letter F)

sangaku shinko (sahn-gah-koo shin-koh): a spiritual tradition centered around the mountains (Please see letter F)

sashiko (sah-shee-koh): a type of stitching on Japanese quilts (Please see letter Q)

Seimei Handan (say-may hahn-dahn): a system of studying names (Please see letter N)

Setsubun (set-soo-bun): a February festival that celebrates the division between winter and spring (Please see letter L)

shamisen (shah-mee-sen): a traditional musical instrument with three strings like a banjo (Please see letter D)

Shinkansen (shin-kahn-sen): the bullet train, the world's first high-speed train (Please see letter B)

Shinto (shin-toh): one of Japan's two major religions (Please see letter R)

shogun (shoh-gun): the feudal lords (Please see letters E & S)

shojo (shoh-joh): manga for girls (Please see letter M)

shonen (shoh-nen): manga for boys (Please see letter M)

Shogatsu (shoh-gah-tsoo): the festival celebrating New Year's Day (Please see letter L)

tabi (tah-bee): split-toe socks (Please see letter K)

torii (toh-ree-ee): a gate at a Shinto shrine, a bird perch (Please see letter R)

Ukiyo-e (oo-kee-o-yay): a style of Japanese painting (Please see letter U)

waka (wah-kah): a form of poetry utilizing five lines (Please see letter H)

zori (zoh-ree): traditional sandals, also called *gela* (Please see letter K)